The Phoenix Living Poets

ROOT AND BRANCH

ROOT AND BRANCH

by

Jon Stallworthy

CHATTO AND WINDUS

THE HOGARTH PRESS

1969

Published by
Chatto and Windus Ltd
with The Hogarth Press Ltd
42 William IV Street
London WC2
*
Clarke, Irwin and Co Ltd
Toronto

SBN 7011 1412 6

Printed in Great Britain by
William Lewis (Printers) Limited
Cardiff

Acknowledgements

Acknowledgements are due to the editors of the following anthologies and periodicals in which some of these poems first appeared: *Agenda, Beliot Poetry Journal, Commonwealth Poems of Today* (John Murray), *Critical Quarterly, The Draconian, The Dublin Magazine, Encounter, English, Extra Verse, Ikon, The Listener, The London Magazine, London Magazine Poems* (Alan Ross), *The Massachusetts Review* (U.S.A.), *Men and Machines* (Ginn), *New Measure, New Poems—1967* (Hutchinson), *The New Statesman, The New York Times* (U.S.A.), *The Oxford Magazine, Oxford New Writing* (Pergamon Press), *Outposts, Poetry Ireland, Poetry 1967, Poetry Northwest* (U.S.A.), *The Poetry Review, Resurgence, The Review, The Review of English Literature, The Sewanee Review, The Sunday Times, The Times Literary Supplement* and *The Transatlantic Review*; also to the Argo Record Company, the producer of 'The Living Poet' programme of the B.B.C., and the editors of the *Exeter Book* and *Turret Book* series who published groups of these poems in pamphlet form.

'Elm End' was awarded second prize in the 1965 Guinness Poetry Competition.

For Margaret and Geoffrey Keynes

and a house of more books than bricks
one book more. Not one to stand
with the gold-shouldered folio spines
of your first friends, the Donnes and Brookes
that fifteen years ago shook a boy's hand.

On how many Friday nights since then
has your front door sheared from my back
the shadow of London. Shadows
are smaller here: as of a pen
across a page, or branches black
on a lawn, lengthening as the light goes.

Last again of the village lights
this lamp in whose blond tent we talk
of the blackberry crop; of your
new Palmer; of my new playwrights
and poets; of an oak's cracked fork—
to be felled tomorrow with the re-set saw.

Grandchildren, come for Sunday lunch,
find us in the garden. They will learn
why all your trees bear fruit, perceive
the root's relation to the branch;
as I have done, who in return
bring you my thin crop hidden among leaves.

Contents

A True Confession

'Truth's a dog must to kennel'

The truth, the whole truth always
and nothing but the truth
ran like a tune through my schooldays,
a theme-song from the myth

of Gawayn and Galahad
and the high court of Arthur,
when Truth and Untruth, Good and Bad
wore different armour.

Truth as the order of the day
worked like a charm at first:
the boys that lied or ran away
always came off worst.

The primary abstractions
in conflict at that range
shivered their swords but broke no bones.
How soon perspectives change,

armour spits blood, true and untrue
look the one colour.
I learnt, after a clash or two,
truth was a killer

and killers must be locked away.
Locking him out of sight
has changed the order of the day
to the order of the night:

when into freedom tunnelling
through my sleep, the truth
breaks from its cell; incites the tongue
to mutiny in my mouth.

All night long the elaborate
armour of self-deceit —
forged so cunningly plate by plate —
falls bloodied at my feet.

Stepping at daybreak out of the lies
of friendship, lies of love,
expedient hypocrisies —
shield gone and visor, glove

struck off — here I unsheathe my pen,
resolved that if it miss
the truth I will begin again:
and lie even in this.

For poets are liars. Their lives
scan less than their smooth
confessions. But now and then our lies
betray us into truth.

Identity Parade

So, you have noticed: I am not
the man he was — the big-shot

captain of the First XV.
His jersey, cramped in polythene,

glows in my cupboard but is half
my size. Your photograph

shows someone else of the same name
confident before the big game.

He knows who he is and where he
is heading, but wouldn't know me

from 22925028,
the subaltern in a slouch hat.

His company in single file
threaded on a compass needle

stitch the map. He leads. He knows
at each river-bank the shallows

from the stream. If, as you tell
me, once I knew him well

we grew apart many years back.
These mornings at the eight o'clock

identity parade I am
a stranger to myself; the sum

of many strangers, who today —
since I have lost their way —

reproach me to my face. You should
get up and go shouts the blood

in my wrist — is it theirs or mine?
Without touchline or gridline

where should I go? Towards that still
mythical stranger whose stare will

appraise — commend or deride —
my choice. I can decide. Decide.

Bread

Breadboard and loaf
waiting for breakfast —
one of the facts of life

not commonly discussed.
Grain white as balsa wood,
bark-wrinkled crust,

give off a good
smell, sweet as cut timber.
This is the body of God

pierced, broken on timber.
Laying the breadknife down
I remember

stick limbs and hunger-blown
bellies; the aftermath
of drought, flood flotsam, cyclone

fodder. And sawdust crams my mouth.

The Postman

Satchel on hip
the postman goes
from doorstep to doorstep
and stooping sows

each letterbox
with seed. His right
hand all the morning makes
the same half circle. White

seed he scatters,
a fistful of
featureless letters
pregnant with ruin or love.

I watch him zig-
zag down the street
dipping his hand in that big
bag, sowing the cool, neat

envelopes which
make *twenty-one*
unaccountably rich,
twenty-two an orphan.

I cannot see
them but I know
others are watching. We
stoop in a row

(as he turns away),
straighten and stand
weighing and delaying
the future in one hand.

A rose is not a rose

in Our Gardening Correspondent's prose.

Crushed between SPIDERMAN'S ACCIDENT
and OSPREYS NESTING it gives off no scent

to sweeten our commuting breath.
On the walk from the station, with

yesterday's record crop of dead
and a column of births folded

under my arm, I enter
Smithfield where the porters saunter

among carcases. Snout by snout
pigs that the cleaver turned inside out

are hung, drawn, and quartered. Parts
I do not recognise loll from carts.

A solitary trotter
blanches as it stains the gutter —

making the eyes recoil, nerves shrink,

Blood is not blood when it is ink.

A Barbican Ash

City pigeons on the air
planing like surfers swirl in their
calm descent, skid on one wing
about a tree where no sapling
was yesterday. Their country cousins,
counties away, now circle in
search of a nest not to be found
between the holed sky and the holed ground.
Like a flag at its masthead frayed
with shot, in this I read
of a tree winched from a wood
to be set in a concrete glade.
Workmen today come packing
its roots with a chemical Spring.

Men are more mobile than trees:
but have, when transplanted to cities,
no mineral extract of manure,
hormone or vitamin to ensure
that their roots survive, carve through the stone
roots, cable roots, strangling my own.

Sensation

Yellow and poster-striped the hornet vans
swarm into view hymning Humanity,
Truth, and the Public Good — their glands
charged with the venom to infect a city.

Summer 1963

Telegrams

When the chrysalis broke
open in her hand
the white, hinged, wings
of the telegram shook,
as if to test the wind
of her altered breathing.

With a street in spate, torrents
of chromium between
my kerb and her doorstep,
I could not read the sentence
she unfolded when
her paper face looked up.

But a kind of love
extended my senses
beyond their frontiers.
I could hear above
the city insect voices —
locusts, jamming my ears

with their calls and the black-
lettered tide
of their wings. Telegrams!
Shortcircuiting the clock —
half the world in one stride —
they travel light as poems.

Heart stammer, hand stammer
printing the air;
the voltage of the nerve
discharged; but somewhere
answering, a tremor
unmistakable as love.

21

An Evening Walk

Taking my evening walk
where flats like liners ride
at anchor on a dark
phosphorus-rippled tide
of traffic, ebbing, flowing,
I heard from a kiosk
a telephone ringing;
from an empty kiosk.

Its dark voice welling up
out of the earth or air
for a moment made me stop,
listen, and consider
whether to break in
on its animal grief.
I could imagine
torrents of relief,

anger, explanation —
'Oh for God's sake' — but I'd
troubles of my own,
and passed on the other side.
All the same I wondered,
with every step I took,
what I would have heard
lifting it from the hook.

As I was returning
after the pubs were shut,
I found the bulb still burning
in the kiosk, but

the dark voice from the dark
had done with ringing:
the phone was off the hook
and like a hanged man swinging.

As Others See Us

She finding on his lips
sour champagne, and he
on her hair confetti,
they enter that eclipse

the novels promise. She
in his eyes, he in hers,
melt as the moon devours
the sun. They do not see —

until a sixth raw sense
nags them to consciousness —
the eye against the glass
cold as a camera lens.

Sickened, they see in this
a creature double-backed
disturbed in a gross act.
The eye blinks, vanishes:

but still the staring pane
holds like a negative
her Adam and his Eve
unparadised again.

Harvest Moon

He at the sill saying
over again, *My God,*
will it ever stop growing? —
a question echoed
by the upturned faces
moonstruck in the road.

Weeks past her waning still
the moon grows. Pores become
pockmarks as her flanks fill,
filling the night sky. *Look,*
London would go under
if her waters broke.

Through porous curtains light
leaks, and through eyelashes
scalds the eye. Last night
she dreamt, as she fell
asleep, of a dark bird
breaking from a bright shell.

Two Hands

My father in his study sits up late,
a pencil nodding stiffly in the hand
that thirteen times between breakfast and
supper led a scalpel an intricate
dance. The phone has sobbed itself to sleep,
but he has articles to read. I curse
tonight, at the other end of the house,
this other hand whose indecisions keep
me cursing nightly; fingers with some style
on paper, elsewhere none. Who would have thought
hands so alike — spade palms, blunt fingers short
in the joint — would have no more in common? All
today, remembering the one, I have watched
the other save no one, serve no one, dance
with this pencil. Hand, you may have your chance
to stitch a life for fingers that have stitched
new life for many. Down the *Lancet* margin
his hand moves rapidly as mine moves slow.
A spasm shakes the phone at his elbow.
The pencil drops: he will be out again.

The Balance of the Mind

The telephone has brought
death to the house,
an obscene fungus
swarming from its root

to the branch in your hand.
Death in its due season
can be the dislocation
of a leaf no wind

tugs from its mooring; breath
can ebb from a cool pillow
calmly. But this was no
such seasonable death.

Spores grapple your ear,
lower into your throat
their rooting tendrils. *Out,*
I say, *into the air* —

before the fungus
cataracts your eye
and the broad lens of sky.
Though earth gape under us

look what it gives back — *live*
buds for leaf-mould. March
has run its colours up the larch.
Grass dances on its grave.

Thistles

Half grown before half seen,
like urchins in armour
double their size they stand
their ground boldly, their keen
swords out. But the farmer
ignores them. Not a hand

will he lift to cut them down:
they are not worth his switch
he says. Uncertain whom
they challenge, having grown
into their armour, each
breaks out a purple plume.

Under this image
of their warrior blood
they make a good death,
meeting the farmer's blade
squarely in their old age.
White then as winter breath

from every white head
a soul springs up. The wind
is charged with spirits: no —
not spirits of the dead
for these are living, will land
at our backs and go

to ground. Farmer and scythe
sing to each other. He
cannot see how roots writhe
underfoot, how the sons
of this fallen infantry
will separate our bones.

The Stone

After the Polish by Zbigniew Herbert

The stone
is a perfect creature

obedient to its own
bounds true to its nature

filled to its firm rind
with a stony meaning

with a scent to remind
no one of anything

to frighten nothing lure
nothing kindle no lust

its coldness and ardour
are dignified and just

I hold it guiltily
in my curved palm

its honourable body
dishonourably warm

stones cannot be tamed
looking at us will lie

to the end with undimmed
unwavering eye

False Alarm

After the Polish by Tymoteusz Karpowicz

The cry and the silence
after the cry turned out
the neighbours, ambulance,

policemen running: but
nobody's head, chest, arm
was bloody or bullet-

plugged. Finding the street calm
the crowd frayed at the fringe,
called it a false alarm —

as if only the tinge
of blood or bullet-singe
below the heart can be
marks of man's agony.

The Almond Tree

I

All the way to the hospital
the lights were green as peppermints.
Trees of black iron broke into leaf
ahead of me, as if
I were the lucky prince
in an enchanted wood
summoning summer with my whistle,
banishing winter with a nod.

Swung by the road from bend to bend,
I was aware that blood was running
down through the delta of my wrist
and under arches
of bright bone. Centuries,
continents it had crossed;
from an undisclosed beginning
spiralling to an unmapped end.

II

Crossing (at sixty) Magdalen Bridge
Let it be a son, a son, said
the man in the driving mirror,
Let it be a son. The tower
held up its hand: the college
bells shook their blessing on his head.

III

I parked in an almond's
shadow blossom, for the tree
was waving, waving me
upstairs with a child's hands.

IV

Up
the spinal stair
and at the top
along
a bone-white corridor
the blood tide swung
me swung me to a room
whose walls shuddered
with the shuddering womb.
Under the sheet
wave after wave, wave
after wave beat
on the bone coast, bringing
ashore — whom?
                    New-
minted, my bright farthing!
Coined by our love, stamped with
our images, how you
enrich us! Both
you make one. Welcome
to your white sheet,
my best poem!

V

At seven-thirty
the visitors' bell
scissored the calm
of the corridors.
The doctor walked with me
to the slicing doors.

His hand upon my arm,
his voice — *I have to tell
you* — set another bell
beating in my head:
your son is a mongol
the doctor said.

VI

How easily the word went in —
clean as a bullet
leaving no mark on the skin,
stopping the heart within it.

This was my first death.
The 'I' ascending on a slow
last thermal breath
studied the man below

as a pilot treading air might
the buckled shell of his plane —
boot, glove, and helmet
feeling no pain

from the snapped wires' radiant ends.
Looking down from a thousand feet
I held four walls in the lens
of an eye; wall, window, the street

a torrent of windscreens, my own
car under its almond tree,
and the almond waving me down.
I wrestled against gravity,

but light was melting and the gulf
cracked open. Unfamiliar
the body of my late self
I carried to the car.

VII

The hospital — its heavy freight
lashed down ship-shape ward over ward —
steamed into night with some on board
soon to be lost if the desperate

charts were known. Others would come
altered to land or find the land
altered. At their voyage's end
some would be added to, some

diminished. In a numbered cot
my son sailed from me; never to come
ashore into my kingdom
speaking my language. Better not

look that way. The almond tree
was beautiful in labour. Blood-
dark, quickening, bud after bud
split, flower after flower shook free.

On the darkening wind a pale
face floated. Out of reach. Only when
the buds, all the buds, were broken
would the tree be in full sail.

In labour the tree was becoming
itself. I, too, rooted in earth
and ringed by darkness, from the death
of myself saw myself blossoming,

wrenched from the caul of my thirty
years' growing, fathered by my son,
unkindly in a kind season
by love shattered and set free

VIII

You turn to the window for the first time.
I am called to the cot
to see your focus shift,
take tendril-hold on a shaft
of sun, explore its dusty surface, climb
to an eye you cannot

meet. You have a sickness they cannot heal,
the doctors say: locked in
your body you will remain.
Well, I have been locked in mine.
We will tunnel each other out. You seal
the covenant with a grin.

In the days we have known one another,
my little mongol love,
I have learnt more from your lips
than you will from mine perhaps:
I have learnt that to live is to suffer,
to suffer is to live.

By Rule of Thumb

Leather and wood and stone —
meeting the grain of my thumb
with as rare a grain of their own —

ratify a treaty made
centuries back between
thumbprint and the print of hide,

the stubborn grain of flint
and the lithe grain of wood.
I track my thumbprint

through its coils. The lifeline
swerving hand over hand
goes to ground in one

clenched on an adze. Roughness
of shaft, blade, thong;
lines travelling to this

glove, pebble, tabletop
I turn towards, turning
from heartache with the sap

shrunk in its severed grain.
So many sinews cut.
Glove and table contain

felled herds and forests, and
a chain-gang hundreds strong
moves when I move my hand.

Glove, paperweight, and table
cut from the running grain
are whole, are serviceable,

and teach me how to take
my soundings with a line
that holds though the heart break.

The Fall of a Sparrow

Who disinherits
the son we endowed in the womb?
If not the hand of chance
dicing with chromosomes,
what strategy of Providence
cost our sparrow his five wits?

The comforters
speak of our windfall as the price
of a poet's licence —
the necessary sacrifice,
a pound of flesh no distance
from the heart. But the heart answers

no. Is a life
in the shadow to be outweighed
by the moving shadow
of a life across a page?
Does Providence sell a sparrow
for a song? Husband and wife

ask one another
the answer they never get right
night after night. Question
and answer turn tail at first light.
A cot shakes, and the fallen sun
rises for father and mother.

At Take-Off

No longer when the lights flick on
No Smoking, Fasten your Seatbelts
that picture — fading as the floor tilts
upward — of the stiff tarpaulin
over me dividing darkness
from darkness, and no stars: instead,
the snapshot of an unscarred head
falling behind me, fatherless.

On the Road

The red lights running my way
keep their distance, hold their fire; the white
blaze from both barrels as they
lunge past. Headlamp and tail-light

switch in the mirror, white to red,
red to white as gears shift down
to overtake. Shot through the head
with lights I sway from town to town.

Red corpuscles, white corpuscles,
thread the branched arteries.
Cramp gnaws my anklebone, worries
the calf-muscle

wired to a pedal. Untuned now
the athlete's pulse stumbles through fat
that once ran steady as the flow
of petrol under my foot.

Cylinders leaping at the swerve
of the road inherit
our animal blood; I hear it
answer the summoning nerve

in other arteries. I have been
how many years on the road?
The dashboard reels off a ribbon
of figures I cannot read

for the ricochet of lights
from windscreen and wet street.
Long enough to remember nights
when blood through all its channels beat

with one current marrying white
and red. The sky over London
burns like my forehead; heat without
energy, light without vision.

Bacillae spawn in the bloodstream,
but the stream has outrun its poisons
before. I thread a fever-dream
of crossroads, straining to read the signs.

Epilogue to an Empire
1600 – 1900
an ode for Trafalgar Day

As I was crossing Trafalgar Square
whose but the Admiral's shadow hand
should tap my shoulder. At my ear:
'You Sir, stay-at-home citizen
poet, here's more use for your pen
than picking scabs. Tell them in England
this: when first I stuck my head in the air,

'winched from a cockpit's tar and blood
to my crow's nest over London, I
looked down on a singular crowd
moving with the confident swell
of the sea. As it rose and fell
every pulse in the estuary
carried them quayward, carried them seaward.

'Box-wallah, missionary, clerk,
lancer, planter, I saw them all
linked like the waves on the waves embark.
Their eyes looked out — as yours look in —
to harbour names on the cabin-
trunks carrying topees to Bengal,
maxims or gospels to lighten a dark

'continent. Blatant as the flag
they went out under were the bright
abstractions nailed to every mast.
Sharpshooters since have riddled most
and buried an empire in their rags —
scrivener, do you dare to write
a little 'e' in the epilogue

42

'to an empire that spread its wings
wider than Rome? They are folded,
you say, with the maps and flags; awnings
and verandahs overrun
by impis of the ant; sun-
downers sunk, and the planters' blood
turned tea or siphoned into rubber saplings.

'My one eye reports that their roads
remain, their laws, their language
seeding all winds. They were no gods
from harnessed clouds, as the islanders
thought them, nor were they monsters
but men, as you stooped over your page
and you and you and these wind-driven crowds

'are and are not. For you have lost
their rhythm, the pulse of the sea
in their salt blood. Your heart has missed
the beat of centuries, its channels
silted to their source. The muscles
of the will stricken by distrophy
dishonour those that bareback rode the crest

'of untamed seas. Acknowledge
their energy. If you condemn
their violence in a violent age
speak of their courage. Mock their pride
when, having built as well, in as wide
a compass, you have none. Tell them
in England this.'
                    And a pigeon sealed the page.

Kathmandu — Kodari

They are building a road out of Kathmandu —
sixty-three miles to be cut with the spade
and five tall bridges to be made
with baskets of cement and bamboo

scaffolding. They are building a road
to Kodari, a high road to be met
with ceremony in Tibet
by the Chungking-Lhasa-Kodari road.

What will they carry, these five tall bridges?
Coolies trudging northward under bales of rice
or troop-filled lorries
travelling south? Periwigged like judges

the Himalayas watch the road-gangs labour.
Today, though the road-gangs seldom look up,
Kangchenjunga wears a black cap:
and the wind from Tibet sweeps like a sabre.

A New Horse for Nepal

Equo ne credite, Teucri.
Quidquid id est, timeo Danaos et dona ferentes.

We come among you with our cameras,
little people of Nepal, and because
they are not carbines you smile at us
out of your carven window-frames and doors.

If they were carbines you would resist us
in a manner becoming your fierce gods,
but nothing so comic can be dangerous,
you think, watching us crouched over tripods.

We bring you the Twentieth Century,
knowledge and power, new lamps for old — neon
to lighten your darkness. We bring you free
samples and trading stamps, nylon, pylon,

and a Hilton half as high as Everest.
No longer to monsoon or the young exposed,
your gods shall have safe conduct to our best
museums, making way for the bulldozed

comfort-stations. Coolie, throw down your pack!
Rickshaw driver, take a Cadillac!
Lama, sell your cymbals, quit your drums:
what need a prayer-wheel when the juke-box comes?

Pagoda gables, we bring you a new horse
more potent than those rampant over us.
Lift up your heads, ye pagoda doors,
lift up your heads for the Mobil Pegasus!

Note: Priapic stallions, rampant and fantastically carved, are a
common feature of temple architecture in the Kathmandu valley

A Prayer to the Virgin

*The Russian Orthodox Greek Catholic Church
of America, which is hoping to buy the icon
The Virgin of Kazan from an Englishwoman for
£178,500, is satisfied that the icon . . . is
the original one from Moscow cathedral.*

THE TIMES
19th November 1963

A refugee finds refuge: San
Francisco takes you in
despite the colour of your skin
and your place of origin,
Black Virgin of Kazan.

When waves over Europe ran
hill-high you crossed them without harm,
your jewelled son upon your arm.
Others were swallowed by the storm,
Black Virgin of Kazan.

Miracle-worker, citizen
of East and West, may those that do
you honour see in you
the mothers that have not come through
miraculously from Kazan.

A greater miracle would be done
if all your diamonds melted
into tears, if all your rubies bled;
and children, everywhere, had bread,
Black Virgin of Kazan.

War Song of the Embattled Finns
1939

Snow inexhaustibly
falling on snow! Those whom
we fight are so many,
Finland so small,
where shall we ever find room
to bury them all?

Sword Music

All that Anglo-Saxon jazz
of *brond on brynie* stuns the ear
attuned to higher frequencies.

But as you wield the words they welded
the great worm bleeds; nor can its venom
scald that sprung edge as it scalded

the smith and the giver of rings.
The consonants keep their balance,
dark shine of the raven's wings.

Byrhtwold over Byrhtnoth:
'Hige sceal þe heardra, heorte þe cenre,
mod sceal þe mare, þe ure maegen lytlað.'

Words so tempered, forged on the tongue
from loyalty, tenacity,
and pride, time can but sharpen. Wrung

from such obsolescent ores,
their words outlast their weapons
and may outlast ours.

'The will shall be harder, courage keener,
Spirit shall grow as our strength falls away.'
                    from 'The Battle of Maldon'

48

A Portrait of Robert Capa

Three eyes in the mirror
behind the bar (one of them shut
since five o'clock) burn and burn out
    in time to the mortar

    like a severed vein
ejaculating on the night
jet after rhythmic jet of light.
    'How did it go?' The brain

    unreels its images
frame by frame: holding to the flash
troops kneeling by a stream to wash
    unfamiliar faces;

    boots on a white road show
their teeth; a corporal on his back
plays with a puppy and a stick.
    'Robert, what'll you do

    when the war is over?'
The third eye lifted in a mute
rejoiner to the gun's salute,
    blinks at the mirror

    before the concussion
succeeds the flash. 'I cover
a war that will never
    be lost, never be won.'

A poem about Poems About Vietnam

The spotlights had you covered [*thunder
in the wings*]. In the combat zones
and in the Circle, darkness. Under
the muzzles of the microphones
you opened fire, and a phalanx
of loudspeakers shook on the wall;
but all your cartridges were blanks
when you were at the Albert Hall.

Lord George Byron cared for Greece,
Auden and Cornford cared for Spain,
confronted bullets and disease
to make their poems' meaning plain;
but you — by what right did you wear
suffering like a service medal,
numbing the nerve that they laid bare,
when you were at the Albert Hall?

The poets of another time —
Owen with a rifle-butt
between his paper and the slime,
Donne quitting Her pillow to cut
a quill — knew that in love and war
dispatches from the front are all.
We believe them, they were there,
when you were at the Albert Hall.

Poet, they whisper in their sleep
louder from underground than all
the mikes that hung upon your lips
when you were at the Albert Hall.

T. E. L.

Speed is the second oldest animal craving
in our nature . . . Every natural man
cultivates the speed that appeals to him.
I have a motor-bike income.

Leader of insurgents he knew too much
of sabotage — raids from within, raids from
behind — to hazard, even in the touch
of hands, an insurrection nearer home.

Heroes he knew from the good books mutiny
against themselves: and when his legs bestrid
the desert ocean, unlike Antony
he let no Cleopatra break his stride

and flaw the epic. After blood and ink
were dry, still he denied the oldest
animal craving. Engine and petrol-tank
pulsing beneath him were sweeter than breast

and thigh: and as boys from the barrack hut
bounced their women, nightly, over the hill
he straddled an ideal more passionate
and in its passion subject to his will.

Embracing, like Hippolytus, a wind
that kissed the lips back from his teeth, he came —
rarest of lovers — to the long-imagined
consummation equal to his dream.

A Word with The Baas

Cecil John Rhodes

Well, my colossus, how do things look
from your view of the world? Is it
only seventy years and a bit,
one man's lifetime, since you shook

your finger at the map and said —
your shadow darkening immense
mountain-cross-hatched continents —
'Africa, I want it red'?

One man's lifetime but many lives,
all tributaries, like your own
turbulent pulse, of that pulse grown
to a river whose dark volume drives

a continent. Africa feeds
off blood like a vampire bat
and is not filled, does not grow fat
though a redcoat regiment bleeds

on the assegai. She can digest
a million head of cattle, mobs,
impis, and you: and still the ribs
tentpole her skin, and still her breast

for all that blood yields only dust
and marketable stones. For these
the white tents swarmed over Kimberley's
kopje, sudden as a locust

plague. Gold reef and diamond,
magnetic under tons of earth,
swung the heads of your oxen north.
Beyond the Limpopo, beyond

the Zambezi, Sheba at noon
hung in a golden haze. The nights'
slow-marching glacier of lights
miraged the mines of Prester John.

But farm by *kraal,* as the Mafeking road
took you to its heart, the *Boy's Own* dream
of bullion ripened to a dream
of land. No frontiers furrowed

your mind's map — only the railway
trained on the north. Your skeleton key
to open Africa from sea
to sea ground in the lock. Today

in your Matopo eerie shut
forever at your own request,
are we to think you cursed or blessed
having a god's perspective but

impotence more than man's? No tongue
for thunder now, no thunderbolt
telegrams crossing the *veld*:
the market beared, concessions wrung

from stubborn *kraals.* All that is ended.
Felled or furled its Union Jacks,
Africa, many-coloured, mocks
your vision: 'Red, I want it red

from Cairo to the Cape,' you said.
Do your eyes ache for lids? Sharpeville,
Katanga, Ruanda, mingle
their streams. The river mounts. The red

river threatens its banks of flesh.
Pray that the gods, my colossus,
electing mercy, may be less
ironic than to grant your wish.

A Letter from Berlin

My dear,
                    Today a letter from Berlin
where snow — the first of '38 — flew in,
settled and shrivelled on the lamp last night,
broke moth wings mobbing the window. Light
woke me early, but the trams were late:
I had to run from the Brandenburg Gate
skidding, groaning like a tram, and sodden
to the knees. Von Neumann operates at 10
and would do if the sky fell in. They lock
his theatre doors on the stroke of the clock —
but today I was lucky: found a gap
in the gallery next to a chap
I knew just as the doors were closing. Last,
as expected, on Von Showmann's list
the new vaginal hysterectomy
that brought me to Berlin.
                                Delicately
he went to work, making from right to left
a semi-circular incision. Deft
dissection of the fascia. The blood-
blossoming arteries nipped in the bud.
Speculum, scissors, clamps — the uterus
cleanly delivered, the pouch of Douglas
stripped to the rectum, and the cavity
closed. Never have I seen such masterly
technique. 'And so little bleeding!' I said
half to myself, half to my neighbour.
                                        'Dead',
came his whisper. 'Dont be a fool'
I said, for still below us in the pool

of light the marvellous unhurried hands
were stitching, tying the double strands
of catgut, stitching, tying. It was like
a concert, watching those hands unlock
the music from their score. And at the end
one half expected him to turn and bend
stiffly towards us. Stiffly he walked out
and his audience shuffled after. But
finishing my notes in the gallery
I saw them uncover the patient: she
was dead.

      I met my neighbour in the street
waiting for the same tram, stamping his feet
on the pavement's broken snow, and said:
'I have to apologize. She was dead,
but how did you know?' Back came his voice
like a bullet ' — saw it last month, twice.'

Returning your letter to an envelope
yellower by years than when you sealed it up,
darkly the omens emerge. A ritual wound
yellow at the lip yawns in my hand;
a turbulent crater; a trench, filled
not with snow only, east of Buchenwald.

Elm End

I

Those cherubs on the gate
emasculated by the village boys
are now sole heirs to the estate.

The elms in the avenue,
planted through centuries
one for a daughter, two

for a son, within the year
will carry the timber-
merchant's mark. He walks here

sometimes on Sunday. The rings
on their trunks are numbered:
and a rip-saw sings

in his head seeing columns
of figures march and countermarch.
This Sunday comes

the snow, keeping him indoors:
but it re-vaults the avenue
and for today restores

that manhood the cherubs knew
when a lodge-keeper swung the gate
letting the phaetons through.

II

Don't worry the bell in the porch.
If its tongue is not tied
with rust, it will search

out a ghost from the scullery.
The handle demands both hands:
go in, go up. He will be

pillow-bound in the great bed
under the griffin's eye
that saw his father born, and dead,

and him conceived. His grandmother's
grandmother caged that bird
in its crest, stitching feathers

by candlelight for Charlie
riding to Waterloo.
Under her canopy

the griffin sees not the hollow
trunk, tackled by gravity, but
how far the roots stretch under snow.

III

The fires have fallen. He has drawn
the white acres up to his chin:
fingers grapple the lawn

that once they crawled on. Letting go
can be harder than holding on
or taking hold — as elms ago

the griffin's claw took hold
of these white acres. Letting go
is a language he's too old

to learn. The griffin grips
a scroll inscribed *Hold Fast*
between its talon tips.

Tonight or tomorrow
or tomorrow night
he will cease to echo

the wind in the chimney. Blinds
will be lowered. The snow
will cover his hands.

If then the bulldozer roars
at its kill, he will not hear,
nor see the road-gang's griffin flex its claws.

Auto Da Fe

October, and I learn
from calendars and trees
to be my age — shed, burn
the scented memories

of summer. Too many
summers weighing me down
with unshed letters She
or She sent me, still done

up in ribbon. Ribbon,
permit me. Do you blush
to recall some permission
granted these fingers? 'Hush',

you whisper, letting slip
a blue-veined load
I lifted to my lip
at seventeen. Aloud

I try out her name: *Ann* —
who brought me to my senses —
first shall be first. Come, fan
my flame with your sentences

not for the first time, but
the last! And now, in order
of appearance, each lot
of letters grows a black border.

Angela, Jacqueline,
Astrid, go through the fire

for me. Their smoke gets in
my eyes as they mount the pyre.

The face in each photograph,
aged in a flash, caves in;
the perfect cheekbones slough
the perfect skin.

Who's that behind her? Ouch!
I burnt my fingers, but
never this much!
I can't put myself out!

Oh no! The letters She
sent back shrivel to hot
air! Our ashes mingle; She
loves me, She loves me not.

Hazel, I burn for you!
My life goes up in flames,
a kiss to end and outdo
all . . .
         The shapes of your names

melt in my mouth. Freelance
no longer I take my leave
of you with this last dance.
If you carry my love

in your personal luggage,
more than your ears will burn.
My phoenixes, act your age;
blaze and be reborn.

March Morning, N.W. 3

The fields from Islington to Marylebone,
To Primrose Hill and Saint John's Wood,
Were builded over with pillars of gold,
And there Jerusalem's pillars stood.
WILLIAM BLAKE

A wind that rocked the stems of cranes
and daffodils across the park
snapped the bedroom curtains
in my face, and drills broke up the dark.

Time to step up from underground
time to step out and take the air,
blood whispered, tired of tracking round
that unlit inner circle where

the living ride with the dead
and those now neither who will
be both. The March sun overhead,
turning the tide in vein and tendril,

turned me out of doors; turned my feet
from the pinstripe parallels
of a straight and narrow street
to the path over Primrose Hill.

Fountainheads, sealed with soot, answered
the sun, and I saw their green lips
opened again. Root and bole stirred
to a new pulse bending twig-tips

skyward, building the intricate
cities of summer from a blue-

print of spring. It was half past eight
by the ever-right sun. Below

me London sloughed its winter skin,
smoke coiling westward; to the east
window-scales were golden. In
that moment the snarling drills ceased

and a voice lassooed me. Daffodil-
yellow his helmet, twenty floors high,
he stood on a scaffolding grill
waving a cloud to catch my eye.

And I waved my handkerchief back
(hearing no word of his message
for the drills were ploughing tarmac
again; a terrace's wreckage

turned to a bulldozer's breakfast).
Was he asking the time, mocking
the shine on my trowsers, or just
wishing me luck? *Time to be making*

a fresh start, boyo, I wanted
to say. *Watch how the plane-trees hoist
into leaf the distilled dead —
this year's leaf higher than last.*

*The graveyards of London renew
the middle air; our province; soon
to be theirs, who through nerve circuits now
signal to be hoisted to the sun.*